Tips for Talking about Tough Situations at School

Stella Alexandre & Gene Finney

GOOD APPLE
A Division of Frank Schaffer Publications, Inc.

Editor: Kathleen Hex
Cover Illustration: Photographs by Comstock
Cover Design: Riley Wilkinson

GOOD APPLE

A Division of Frank Schaffer Publications, Inc.
23740 Hawthorne Boulevard
Torrance, CA 90505-5927

Contents

Introduction

In response to many questions asked by colleagues and parents over the years regarding how to address issues of concern to middle grade youngsters, this brief book was written. Between the two authors, we have over sixty-three years in the classroom working with middle-grade students—watching them develop and grow into confident, expressive young people.

We hope we can benefit others with our experience as we share here our techniques for discussing with students the forty topics we have chosen. We hope to help other teachers experience the same success we witnessed with our students. Our experiences were enriched when we recognized the importance of "hearing" the young people in our care and in making them feel good about themselves and secure in their environment.

Although many of the topics discussed with young people included in this book had to be handled quickly, we tried to allow time to discuss these concerns as thoroughly as possible in the classroom setting. We found it beneficial to schedule a time when a designated topic could be thoughtfully discussed in a follow-up activity as well.

Many learning skills were demonstrated by the students as they learned to express themselves in groups both large and small. Over time, students listened to others, cooperated within a group, trusted their own feelings, were able to change their opinions, and recognized the many ways that problems can be resolved.

Our school gave us a very diversified population. Students entered our school from many countries from around the world. This enrollment reflected many different viewpoints, beliefs, and often involved languages other than English.

To handle this diversity, we used humor and understanding and were honest when asking students to share their feelings. There were no judgmental solutions to any of the problems presented. As teachers, we accepted the students' opinions before we ever interjected our guidance.

Even with our combined 63 years of teaching experience, we managed to learn much during our discussions from our students. There were many times when the only positive conclusion from the students' discussions was that the students were given an opportunity to talk openly about their concerns without fear of being judged or graded. Recognizing their own true feelings and seeing these feelings mirrored in some of their friends helped most students to understand that they were not alone or experiencing "bad" or unnatural feelings. This open communication enabled our students to gain much-needed self-esteem and confidence.

We tried to teach our students how to avoid feeling frustrated and angry when no decision could be reached or agreed upon during our discussion of the various delicate topics. The students learned that there are many choices that people make when solving their own problems. This empowerment allowed students to make new choices with newfound confidence. They felt responsible when able to freely express their thoughts and opinions. They also eagerly tried to understand how others were feeling about discussion topics.

When any of the forty topics in this book are introduced to the class, we suggest the following format for these discussions. After the class is assembled, the problem that will be addressed should be read to the entire group. Then the teacher should ask the class to regroup in small numbers; for example, a class of 30 could be divided into five groups of six students each. Each group should be given about five minutes to talk about the topic problem and what they would do to solve it. Then the group meets as a whole class and each group is given a few minutes to share their solutions. The teacher then becomes a secretary and records the students' remarks on the chalkboard for further discussion.

Finally, the teacher should read what has been suggested in this book as a possible solution. These solutions are offered as discussion points only, not as a right response or answer. Other viewpoints should be expressed as well. When diverse opinions are acknowledged, they reinforce our individuality as problem solvers.

A camcorder may be operated by a volunteer to review the discussion sessions. Since most of us are familiar with the talk show format on television, students may welcome the opportunity to participate in this meaningful vehicle for exchange of their ideas.

Whenever possible, the recorded videotape can be reviewed as a class activity. A library system to watch recorded videotapes could be initiated for students who did not participate in the taped presentations. The tapes could also be checked out to other teachers or parents who wish to see how children have learned to acknowledge others and their voiced opinions.

We also suggest a free choice period when a student may choose to do one of the following activities to conclude a discussion around any topic. A greater variety of suggested activities also accompanies each individual problem.

1. Design a poster, banner, or draw a cartoon relative to the topic
2. Write a paragraph about the topic
3. Role play the characters depicted by the problem
4. Write a solution that students would choose for themselves for the problem
5. Write a poem relative to the topic
6. Research the subject and present findings to the class
7. Find a book or selection that gives more information about the problem

The goals in this book that we focused on developing are more intangible than concrete. They are:

- Learning to listen to others
- Cooperating within a group
- Solving conflicts in a non-violent manner
- Trusting one's own feelings
- Developing the ability to change one's opinion
- Recognizing the many ways problems are perceived... and solved
- Recognizing feelings of anger and frustration
- Acquiring self-confidence
- Increasing verbal skills

It is our belief that most middle graders' problems can be discussed openly without fear of punishment or shame and at the same time encourage positive problem solving and listening behaviors. Let's talk about issues with our students—and improve their self-esteem, values, and character skills in the process!

Topic 1: Feeling Left Out

Issue for Discussion

When I don't get chosen to be in a class play, on a team, or other activity at school, I feel that nobody likes me or that I'm not as good as everyone else. How can I get over this feeling? What can I do?

Group Discussion of Possible Solutions

Have students discuss their responses to the above issue and questions. Then lead the following discussion: Many times we're not chosen to participate in certain activities, but this doesn't mean that nobody likes us or that we're not as good as everyone else. You can help your students get over this feeling if you encourage them to volunteer to work with their classmates in other important ways if they are not selected or chosen to participate in an event or activity. There are many things that need to be done in a play or on a team to make the team or group successful. Encourage students to express an interest or willingness to do anything to help or contribute to the group. They might sell tickets, paint posters, collect props, usher or do any other duties that are necessary to put together a successful show or presentation. Their worth will be recognized and valued.

Suggested Activities

1. Have students organize a talent show that can be performed for other classes. Emphasize the need for everyone to cooperate on the logistics of the presentation. Remember, everyone has a talent. Some students have a talent for decorating scenery, others for emceeing, others for performing. Everyone's contribution should be valued.
2. As a homework assignment, students can select a poem to memorize and present to the class. Encourage students to use props, puppets, or costumes to dramatize their selection for a younger audience.

Values and Character Skills Emphasized in This Discussion

- Working Cooperatively with Others
- Sense of Community or Shared Responsibility
- Positive Self-Esteem

Topic 2: Managing Homework Assignments

Issue for Discussion

When I'm given a class assignment that is to be completed at home, I sometimes don't know where to go for help or even how to begin. I wait until the last minute and then I get really stressed and worried and end up getting a poor grade on my assignment. What am I supposed to do?

Group Discussion of Possible Solutions

Ask students to share their ideas for managing homework assignments. Have them jot down tips or suggestions to share with the class. Then explain to students that waiting until the last minute will almost always create anxiety or extra stress when working on a homework assignment. Remind students of the benefit of scheduling work early; breaking the assignment into manageable tasks; asking for clarification if something is not understood; knowing when to ask for help; and managing time to complete an assignment.

Suggested Activities

1. Role play talking with several different adults (parents, teachers, etc.)—all revolving around asking for support for homework assignments. Vary the situations: Asking teacher to clarify assignment; asking parents for opinions/support; asking librarian for references/sources, and so on.
2. With the help of the class, compile a list of community resources that students have access to as they work on class assignments: colleges, libraries, planetarium, museums, and so on. Encourage students to make use of these resources as they work on class assignments. Encourage students to view all community resources as support for homework.
3. Encourage students to keep an assignment calendar and involve/inform parents *early* regarding assignment due dates.

Values and Character Skills Emphasized in This Discussion

- Managing a Task
- Responsibility for Completing an Assignment
- Asking for Help or Support When Needed

Topic 3: Can't Do Anything Right

Issue for Discussion

When I was younger, my teachers and friends all seemed to like me—it seemed I could do no wrong. Now it seems that I can't do anything right! No matter how hard I try! How can I go back to the way it used to be?

Group Discussion of Possible Solutions

Ask students to talk about why, when, or if they sometimes feel they can't do anything right. Have them list things they could improve on or do better. Have them list things that they already do very well. Then continue with the following discussion: It's not unusual when things are not going well to feel as though we can't do anything right. Discuss with students how frustration can contribute to feelings of inadequacy. Help students separate legitimate things to improve on from positive qualities about themselves. Discuss why students sometimes feel they do everything wrong.

Suggested Activities

1. Have students cut out words from newspapers or magazines that they believe can be used to describe themselves. Provide students with a banner on which these words can be pasted. Encourage students to share their feelings, if they wish, or keep them private.
2. Have each student make a list of things that make them feel good about themselves. Glue these phrases or words on a piece of construction paper that is decorated with images that reflect self-pride, self-worth, or self-esteem.
3. Have students list teachers, parents, grandparents, siblings, or friends who have made them feel good about something that they did or said.

Values and Character Skills Emphasized in This Discussion

- Respect for Self
- Confidence
- Positive Self-Esteem

Topic 4: Sharing Secrets

Issue for Discussion

Have you ever told someone a secret—something that you didn't want others to know? Then you found out later that your secret was shared or told. How did you feel?

Group Discussion of Possible Solutions

Encourage students to share experiences about trust, friendship, loyalty and the risks involved in keeping and sharing secrets. Discuss why some secrets should be shared and why others shouldn't. As a group, discuss how to safely share information with others, while protecting one's own privacy. Discuss, too, why some secrets must be shared to protect the safety of others. Then follow up with the following discussion: Some people feel a sense of power in knowing someone else's secret. When they want to impress someone else with their power, they give the secret away. Almost everyone has been disappointed at one time or another by a shared secret. It is fair to feel disappointed by a friend or family member who shares a secret that you asked him or her not to share. Discuss students' feelings about situations where secrets were shared by trusted others.

Suggested Activities

1. Encourage students to describe a situation in which a secret was shared that put them in an uncomfortable or compromising situation. Role play how this situation could be resolved without losing face or respect for self.
2. For a period of one week, encourage students to tally the number of secrets shared with them by friends or acquaintances. Graph the results daily. Graph, too, how many of the shared secrets were later revealed to others. Discuss what students learn about themselves from their graphed results.

Values and Character Skills Emphasized in This Discussion

- Trustworthiness
- Protection of Self
- Responsibility to Do What Is Right

Topic 5: Jealousy

Issue for Discussion

My friends and teachers pay more attention to my best friend than they do to me. I feel like everyone goes out of their way to be nice to my friend, but they do nothing to be nice to me. I sometimes feel like I hate my friend for being so well-liked. Am I bad for having these feelings?

Group Discussion of Possible Solutions

Jealousy can be a very powerful emotion for adolescents. Ask students to offer examples and solutions for dealing with hypothetical episodes of jealousy. Discuss with students how they do have choices they can make when they find that they feel jealous: discuss the feelings of jealousy with their friends and family; step away from the situation that is making them feel jealous and then look at that situation unemotionally; or choose to somehow alter or change the situation to reduce their feelings of jealousy. Helping students understand why they feel the way they do can be helpful, too.

Suggested Activities

1. Have students role play a variety of "jealous" situations and ask for student participation in resolving the conflicts. Or have students dramatize common jealous scenes using puppets.
2. Have students write a story about a personal experience with jealousy. What happened? How was the situation resolved?

Values and Character Skills Emphasized in This Discussion

- Conflict Resolution
- Communication
- Anger Management

Topic 6: Exaggerating the Truth

Issue for Discussion

Sometimes I pretend to have more things—-records, money, friends, and so on—than I really do. I stretch the truth just a little. Is this a bad thing to do?

Group Discussion of Possible Solutions

Ask students to give examples of times they've "stretched the truth" or told "little white" lies. Discuss whether this behavior is appropriate. Discuss why students may have felt it was necessary to "stretch the truth." Follow up with this discussion: We sometimes wrongly think others will be impressed with our possessions and perhaps like us better if we have more of something than we really do. Some people believe that they are successful *only* if they accumulate and possess many things. Explain to students that most people will like them for what they are and not for what they have or do. When students find themselves pretending to have more than they do, remind them that an OKAY person doesn't need to convince others with "stretched" truths.

Suggested Activities

1. On a large sheet of construction paper have students make a collage of pictures of things or characteristics that they wish they could have or be. Encourage students to share their wishes with the class. Discuss which wishes or objects are attainable.
2. Have students make a collage of words or pictures of things that they value about themselves.
3. Read and discuss a story of someone who has learned acceptance of self.

Values and Character Skills Emphasized in This Discussion

- Acceptance of Self
- Telling the Truth
- Positive Self-Esteem

Topic 7: Death of a Classmate

Issue for Discussion

A few weeks ago, a classmate of mine died. I've been feeling very sad since his death. I've felt angry and scared, too. Why am I still so upset and when will I start to feel okay again?

Group Discussion of Possible Solutions

Talk to students about the stages of grief. Talk about their classmate who has died. Talk, too, about the students' fears and feelings. Then continue with this discussion: Explain to students that feeling empty, sad, angry, and scared are natural emotions to feel when someone they know has died. People experience grief in different ways and they recover from their grief at different paces. Grief almost always moves in predictable stages—all natural and all necessary to healing our emotions.

Suggested Activities

1. Have students make a collage that celebrates their friendship and feelings about their classmate who has died. The class may wish to share their collage with the rest of the school or with their classmate's family.
2. Encourage the class to openly share their feelings and memories about their classmate.

Values and Character Skills Emphasized in This Discussion

- Compassion for Others
- Healthy Expression of Grief
- Optimism

Topic 8: Good Manners

Issue for Discussion

I like going to my friend's house because his family is really nice and they always make me feel welcome. One day after school, I was at my friend's house and offered a snack. Instead of saying "No, thank you!" I just said, "No." I didn't mean to be rude or offend my friend's family, but I think I did. Is there anything I can do?

Group Discussion of Possible Solutions

Discuss with students behaviors that represent good manners and behaviors that seem rude. Encourage students to practice good manners with friends, siblings, salespeople, the elderly, and others, each and every day. Discuss the following with students: Although some days it may feel like you are the rudest person in the world, you haven't committed any crime—you've simply made a small mistake and forgotten the rules of good behavior. Remind students that it is polite to say "No, thank you" when something is offered and refused and "Yes, please" or "Yes, thank you" when something is accepted. Suggest alternate behaviors to show consideration of others or actions that demonstrate sincerity and goodwill.

Suggested Activities

1. Brainstorm with the class examples of what they consider to be good manners. List these suggestions on the chalkboard. Ask students to practice these behaviors often.
2. Place 3" x 5" cards in a box or bag with examples of good and bad manners and have each student choose one to illustrate. Use the examples to make a class book that can be shared with other students.

Values and Character Skills Emphasized in This Discussion

- Respect for Others' Feelings
- Consideration for Others
- Social Competence

Topic 9: Hypocritical Behavior

Issue for Discussion

I sometimes get confused when I'm told I should act in a certain way, then I see other people doing just the opposite. For example, my older brother tells me *not* to play with certain friends because they use bad words. I hear *his* friends using the same language, yet he hasn't changed any of his friends. Why is it different for him than it is for me?

Group Discussion of Possible Solutions

Have students define the word *hypocrite* and then share acts of hypocrisy that they have seen in and out of school. Specifically discuss how circumstances of the above situation are different for the older brother than they are for the younger. Should they be? Is being older an advantage for the older brother? Might expectations be different for people of different ages? What is hypocritical and what isn't?

Suggested Activities

1. Have students share examples of situations where they are allowed to say or experience what younger bothers or sisters are not. Is this hypocritical?
2. Have students role play a number of acts of hypocrisy—some real and others that may not be hypocritical. Discuss the differences between the two.

Values and Character Skills Emphasized in This Discussion

- Setting Standards for Self
- Respecting Authority
- Independent Thinking

Topic 10: Copying Homework

Issue for Discussion

I have a friend who copies my homework almost every day. If I object, he says I'm overreacting and not much of a friend. I am angry that my friend is getting credit for my hard work. What can I do?

Group Discussion of Possible Solutions

Ask students how far they should "go" for a friend? What is good for friendship and what is not? What can you ask of a friend? When might you be asking for too much? Follow the student discussion with the following: In the above example, the one friend needs to tell the other friend that he is capable of doing his own work. If the "copying" friend chooses to end the friendship over this, then he wasn't much of a friend to begin with. By encouraging the friend to do his own assignments, the one friend is actually doing his other friend a big favor. He's telling him that he is smart enough to earn good grades by himself. Another option: The two friends might form a study partnership that could be fun and beneficial for both.

Suggested Activities

1. Have students choose a partner with whom they will work together on a class assignment. Encourage students to share their efforts and the outcome of their joint assignment. Stress how combined effort can sometimes produce better results.
2. Arrange a class debate on the topic "Should Each Student Be Responsible for His/Her Own Work?" Pro and Con teams can articulate their positions.

Values and Character Skills Emphasized in This Discussion

- Conflict Resolution
- Responsibility
- Problem Solving

Topic 11: Feeling Sad All the Time

Issue for Discussion

I have a friend who almost always seems unhappy. When I ask him what is wrong, he says, "Nothing." Being with him makes me sad. I worry about him, but I find I don't want to be around him when he's "down." What am I supposed to do?

Group Discussion of Possible Solutions

Ask students how they would handle a situation similar to the one described above. Then discuss the following: If a friend were depressed or sad all the time, a parent or teacher should be told. A depressed friend may need someone to talk to in order to feel better. The best thing you can do for a friend who is sad is get help and offer your support.

Suggested Activities

1. Ask a mental health practitioner to come to class to talk about adolescent depression—how to recognize the signs of depression and how to help.
2. Invite parents of children in school to class to discuss with students the importance of sharing warning signs about depression or any other information affecting the safety of their children to school officials. Stress that alerting parents or teachers to possible trouble is not "tattling," but instead, responsible behavior.

Values and Character Skills Emphasized in This Discussion

- Compassion for Others
- Responsibility
- Moral Courage

Topic 12: Stealing

Issue for Discussion

If I see someone stealing, what am I supposed to do? What if that someone is my friend?

Group Discussion of Possible Solutions

Have students imagine a society where stealing is condoned. What would be the consequences? Follow this discussion with the following: In almost every society, stealing is considered wrong. Little acts of stealing can become a habit that later grows into a very serious problem. If you are aware that stealing is happening, you should report what you know to your teacher or a counselor. You may be doing the "thief" a favor in the long run. Discuss with students how this might be so.

Suggested Activities

1. Invite a retail store representative or a police officer to class to discuss the consequences of stealing. Discuss how theft causes all of us many problems.
2. Discuss how theft causes the thief and everyone else to pay higher retail prices.

Values and Character Skills Emphasized in This Discussion

- Honesty
- Integrity
- Responsibility to Community

Topic 13: Expectations

Issue for Discussion

I sometimes feel that others have expectations of me that I cannot live up to. I also sometimes feel pressured to do or be things I don't want to do or be. What am I supposed to do?

Group Discussion of Possible Solutions

Discuss expectations that are healthy and normal. Discuss expectations that are stressful or annoying. Then continue with the following discussion: We all sometimes feel expectations that anger or even frighten us. Talk to your teachers, coaches, or parents about expectations that are realistic for you, as well as expectations you wish to set for yourself as you grow older.

Suggested Activities

1. Set up the classroom in a talk show format. Appoint an interviewer to discuss the topic "Expectations—How to Effectively Deal with Them." Ask for volunteers from your "audience" (class) to be interviewed. Begin the discussion by asking, "Has anyone here ever been expected to do or be something they didn't want to do or be?" Encourage free discussion.
2. Invite a coach from the school to discuss with students the positive and negative results of having expectations in sports. Invite a teacher from the school to discuss with students the positive and negative results of having academic expectations.

Values and Character Skills Emphasized in This Discussion

- Confidence
- Being True to Self
- Positive Self-Esteem

Topic 14: Bragging

Issue for Discussion

I have a problem in one of my classes. There is a student in this class who is driving me crazy. She always goes on and on about the *wonderful* things that she does and the *wonderful* things that she *has*. I really find her bragging about herself annoying. What can I do?

Group Discussion of Possible Solutions

Ask students to consider why someone might be a braggart. When is bragging extreme and when is bragging acceptable? Then follow up with this discussion: A person who brags excessively will continue to do so until there is no one left to listen. You can help yourself and the person bragging by politely excusing yourself from a conversation where bragging is getting excessive. Bragging in class can be addressed by asking all students to facilitate discussions, clearly stating the order in which speakers will be recognized. Your braggart may get the message that her classmates also have valid experiences worthy of an audience. If a braggart continues to dominate the group, more drastic measures may be in order. A discussion of different viewpoints is both enlightening and provides an understanding of the diversity in our own community.

Suggested Activities

1. Have students use puppets or make puppets during a class art period that can be used to act out the roles of several braggarts. Ask viewers to critique the dramatic performance.
2. Students might like to role play a television or movie character who is also a braggart. Discuss this character's behavior as a group.

Values and Character Skills Emphasized in This Discussion

- Listening to Others
- Valuing Others
- Problem Solving

Topic 15: Speaking in Front of Others

Issue for Discussion

When I have to give an oral report in front of the class, I can get so nervous that I feel as though I am going to get sick. Is there something wrong with me and what can I do?

Group Discussion of Possible Solutions

Ask students to share personal experiences with public speaking. Watch a video of several polished speakers. Discuss the characteristics of a polished presentation and a confident presenter. Follow up with this discussion: Most of your classmates probably feel the same way that you do when it comes to speaking in front of others. We all feel anxiety and some pressure when speaking before friends or even strangers—so much so that it can make many of us feel ill. Some of the world's most famous singers and actors have also felt this way before giving a performance. One thing that you can do is talk to your teacher about your feelings. He or she may give you some suggestions that will make an oral presentation more interesting or humorous. Another thing you can do is prepare your presentation carefully. Then practice, practice, practice, giving your report aloud to others. Record yourself, watch your recording, then critique your performance. Here's another important tip: You will almost always feel more confident if you speak about something you know or believe in.

Suggested Activities

1. Invite students to begin their preparation for giving an oral report by making a tape recording (audio or video) of a selected poem or story. Encourage students to practice reading the poem or story aloud several times first. Then tape the students. Have students play back the tapes to evaluate their performances. Discuss the value of practice as a way of dealing with the difficulty of delivering an oral report before an audience.
2. Encourage students to have parents, grandparents, or friends critique a report or presentation before making the actual class presentation.

Values and Character Skills Emphasized in This Discussion

- Empathy
- Confidence
- Perseverance

Topic 16: Not Eating Well at School

Issue for Discussion

I generally do not like school lunches and find myself either not eating at all or eating only snacks that are not good for me. I know these habits are not healthy. What am I supposed to do?

Group Discussion of Possible Solutions

Ask students to investigate foods that are healthy and nutritious and foods that surprisingly are not. Then discuss the following: More and more school lunch programs are offering healthy food options for students' varied tastes. Unhealthy snacks often have more calories than a body can burn, resulting in weight gain and poor nutrition. Have students suggest salad bar or other options for school lunches to the school lunch supervisor. Encourage students to choose from among the healthy and nutritious food options discovered in their nutrition research.

Suggested Activities

1. Invite a local dietitian to class to give a short presentation on healthy food choices that could be recommended to the school lunch program supervisor as luncheon options.
2. Help students create a class mural of magazine pictures of foods they would eat at lunch. Have students do a nutrition analysis of these foods and critique their value as part of a nutritious school lunch program.

Values and Character Skills Emphasized in This Discussion

- Taking Care of One's Body
- Making Healthy Choices
- Cooperation

Topic 17: Violence at School

Issue for Discussion

I know there are some students at school who carry knives and other weapons. I am afraid of these students and worry that someone, including myself, could get hurt. What am I supposed to do?

Group Discussion of Possible Solutions

Ask students to identify ways to avoid becoming a victim of school or other violence. Discuss responsible protective behaviors, as well as the students' own role in providing a safe school environment. Follow up with this discussion: Violence in our schools is a serious national problem. Recent statistics show that nearly 3 million incidents of violent crime occur on or near school grounds every year—not just in big cities, but in middle and elementary schools across the nation. Have students research and work with teachers, parents, and the community to find ways to rid their school of these dangers. Two great resources to help schools, communities, and students are: Peter Blauvelt's *On Making Your Schools Safe* and Ronald Stephens' *Safe Schools: A Handbook for Violence Prevention.*

Suggested Activities

1. Invite a police officer or a representative from Juvenile Court or a local hospital to school to discuss the dangers of carrying weapons in school and the consequences of violence. Ask the guest speaker to offer suggestions for keeping your school and community safe from violence.
2. Have students evaluate their school's overall climate for safety. Are the grounds safe and well-lighted? Are students respectful of diversity? Ask students to look into programs like anger management, student mediation, or other peaceful resolution programs.

Values and Character Skills Emphasized in This Discussion

- Self-Preservation
- Responsibility for Community
- Conflict Resolution

Topic 18: New Clothes for School

Issue for Discussion

I wish I had nicer clothes for school. What would you suggest I do?

Group Discussion of Possible Solutions

Ask students to discuss the pros and cons of spending lots of money on clothes for school. Discuss, too, what they consider "excessive"? Ask students' opinion of wearing uniforms at school. Discuss the pros and cons of wearing school uniforms. Solicit opinions from parents and teachers, too. Then discuss the following: Often what we wear reflects our personalities, our likes, what makes us feel comfortable about ourselves. Discuss with students a healthy balance between being true to ourselves and dressing well for school.

Suggested Activities

1. Invite a sales representative from a local clothing store that sells clothes to young people to make a short presentation on tips for buying clothes at reasonable prices.
2. Ask students to interview their parents about fashionable clothes they wore when they were young and in school. If available, share parents' pictures of the clothing they wore with the class.

Values and Character Skills Emphasized in This Discussion

- Positive Self-Esteem
- Independent Thinking
- Problem Solving

Topic 19: School Bully

Issue for Discussion

There's a boy in my class who has a reputation for being a bully. I try to avoid him, but he usually catches up with me when I'm on my way home from school. He's bigger than I am and I'm afraid of him. What am I supposed to do?

Group Discussion of Possible Solutions

Discuss with students ways they can avoid a bully's abuse. Then discuss the following: School bullies should not be taken lightly. Studies show that former school bullies often end up as future criminals. Young bullies in school today may also be carrying weapons. Bullies are a common phenomenon in the middle grades—and middle grade students are being victimized more frequently than ever before. If someone is bullying you, don't be ashamed and try to hide it—instead bring the bully's behavior out in the open. Tell your parents or your teacher. Taking no action can escalate the victimization. Bullies need to be confronted and helped.

Suggested Activities

1. Have students write to the National School Safety Center (4165 Thousands Oaks Blvd., Suite 290, Westlake Village, CA 91362) for information on bully behavior and how to deal with bullies in your school.
2. Have students research ways to "bullyproof" their school. Encourage an open campaign against "bully" behavior.

Values and Character Skills Emphasized in This Discussion

- Self-Preservation
- Conflict Resolution
- Courage

Topic 20: Too Small for School Sports

Issue for Discussion

I am very short for my age and wonder if I am too small to participate in sports at school.

Group Discussion of Possible Solutions

Have students discuss how physical size affects performance in sports. Can an athlete be too short? Can an athlete be too tall? Does physical size affect one's level of talent for sports? Then encourage the following discussion: It should give students some comfort to know that some of the world's greatest athletes are not very tall; in fact, some are even short. Regardless of your students' current height, or even their future height as adults, they can still achieve success in both life and sports. Have students discuss how.

Suggested Activities

1. Invite a school nurse or a local doctor to come speak to the class about physical growth—how it varies among individuals and how it is influenced by environment and heredity.
2. Invite a coach or sports trainer to come speak to the class about the varied physical sizes of famous athletes or athletes they have known.

Values and Character Skills Emphasized in This Discussion

- Respect for Our Differences
- Positive Self-Esteem
- Self-Confidence

Topic 21: Teacher's Pet

Issue for Discussion

I have a teacher who tells me that I am one of her best students. She lets me have lots of choices in class and gives me assignments that help her. The other kids are beginning to call me "teacher's pet." I worry that the other students will not like me if I continue to do well in this teacher's class. What can I do?

Group Discussion of Possible Solutions

Ask students to define the meaning of the term "teacher's pet." When is this label appropriate? When might it be unfair? Then discuss the following: Capable students are often labeled a "teacher's pet"—often because they do well in school, are helpful to the teacher, or in some cases, are treated preferentially. Most students are great helpers when given a chance. They can tutor on computers, read with a student, do problem solving, work puzzles, correct papers, and so on. By encouraging all students to help and try harder in school, there will be less of an opportunity to label any one student a "teacher's pet."

Suggested Activities

1. Make a list of things than can be done in the classroom by the students. Invite students to sign up for these assignments on a weekly basis. Suggest that all students share in helping with classroom duties.
2. Just because individuals volunteer to help in the classroom, does this make them a teacher's pet? Encourage a discussion of this question.

Values and Character Skills Emphasized in This Discussion

- Helpfulness
- Teamwork
- Positive Self-Esteem

Topic 22: Blaming Others

Issue for Discussion

Whenever things go wrong, I have the bad habit of blaming others for my troubles. For example, yesterday I lost my book and blamed one of my friends for taking it. My friend is very angry with me for accusing her of something she didn't do. What can I do about my problem?

Group Discussion of Possible Solutions

Discuss with students why it is sometimes easier to "blame" others for our troubles than it is to take responsibility for our woes. Ask students to list times when they seem most vulnerable to "blaming" others. Do they see a pattern? What can they do to change this behavior? Then follow up with this discussion: Blaming others when things don't go right is common among people of all ages. However, nothing teaches us faster than lessons painfully learned. Blaming others for our troubles is seldom helpful and often angers others.

Suggested Activities

1. Ask students to write a story about a time that they decided to accept responsibility for something they did or did not do. Why did they choose to take this action?
2. Ask students to choose a partner who might role play a blaming situation. Present the role play to the class.

Values and Character Skills Emphasized in This Discussion

- Taking Responsibility for Self
- Honesty
- Communication

Topic 23: Chatterbox

Issue for Discussion

I'm beginning to hate my favorite class in school—all because of this one student who won't shut up! He keeps talking and talking. Nobody else has a chance to say anything in class. What can I do?

Group Discussion of Possible Solutions

Have students question why someone might "talk and talk" and never listen. Then initiate the following discussion: Most of us at one time or another have run across a person who will not stop talking! A person who doesn't know how to give others a chance to speak can seem really rude! Unfortunately, these people have not learned how to respect others and their opinions. It might be difficult to do, but if possible, ask the "talker" to take a deep breath and give others a chance to talk, too. The art of good conversation is an equal exchange of thoughts and opinions.

Suggested Activities

1. Have students make a tape recording of someone who is a gracious talker and a considerate listener. Ask students to practice both of these admirable characteristics.
2. Have students write about the problem of being a chatterbox and what it means to family and friends.
3. Have students write a humorous story about a talker and illustrate with a cartoon.
4. Have students write about an incident in which a talker causes an accident or missed opportunity.

Values and Character Skills Emphasized in This Discussion

- Cooperation
- Consideration for Others
- Communication

Topic 24: Tagging Along

Issue for Discussion

Sometimes I plan to do things with one of my friends and another friend calls and wants to come along. I like both of my friends, but sometimes my other friend and I just want to do things by ourselves. How can I tell my second friend that I have other plans without hurting her feelings?

Group Discussion of Possible Solutions

Ask students to discuss the responsibilities of friendship, as well as its benefits and rewards. Can a person have several close friends at one time? What is required to keep a friendship going? Follow up with a discussion of the following: People who have many friends have learned the value of setting aside times to be with them. Sometimes activities include many friends, other times activities include only one or two. In the above example, the second friend should be told honestly that plans have already been made, but another time, plans can be made to include her, too.

Suggested Activities

1. Have students keep track of their activities with friends for one month. Practice spending time alone with friends. Other times practice asking friends to join activities already planned.
2. Have students role play situations where an invitation to do something is turned down, as well as a situation when someone is invited to join an activity that is already planned.

Values and Character Skills Emphasized in This Discussion

- Honesty
- Problem Solving
- Communication

Topic 25: New Student

Issue for Discussion

There's a new student at school who seems to have few friends. Is it my responsibility to help this student feel at home?

Group Discussion of Possible Solutions

Ask students to imagine how difficult it would be to leave their friends and move to a new city, home, or school. Ask again if students can imagine how grateful they would feel if the students in their new school made them feel welcome and at home. Have students share suggestions for welcoming a new student to their city, community, and school.

Suggested Activities

1. Have students compile a list of "nice things" they could do for a new student in their school. Invite students to sign up and assume the responsibility for a particular "nice thing" on a given day. These activities could include a tour of the school building, eating lunch with the new student, and accompanying him/her at break. In other words, be a BIG BROTHER or BIG SISTER for the first few days of a new student's experience at school.
2. Invite a new student to share something of his or her background with the class. Ask other students to introduce themselves and share something about themselves with the new student, too.

Values and Character Skills Emphasized in This Discussion

- Friendliness
- Compassion
- Generosity

Topic 26: Respecting Privacy

Issue for Discussion

The other day I opened my friend's locker without her permission and borrowed one of her books. My friend is angry with me and says I had no right to go into her things without her permission. Was I wrong?

Group Discussion of Possible Solutions

Ask students to list times they have felt an invasion of privacy—either at home or at school. Have students talk about how they felt. Then discuss the following: Even good friends respect each other's privacy and possessions. It's best never to take anything from anyone without their permission. Have students discuss inconveniences or negative outcomes that could result from taking something from someone without their permission.

Suggested Activities

1. Have students discuss ways or times they could have been more respectful of another's property.
2. Have students write a story about a time when they were inconvenienced by another's disregard of their personal property.

Values and Character Skills Emphasized in This Discussion

- Respect for Other's Property
- Honesty
- Cooperation

Topic 27: Conversation

Issue for Discussion

Sometimes when I meet someone new, I don't know what to say. I feel awkward and shy. What can I do?

Group Discussion of Possible Solutions

Why might someone feel shy around new people? Why are some people naturally more shy than others? Discuss with students techniques for improving self-confidence in social situations. Then follow up with the following discussion: Most people like to talk about themselves. You will always be safe in an uncomfortable social situation asking questions about someone's interests, hobbies, or activities. When you show a genuine interest in others, they will think you are a special person for being interested in them, too. Remember: A great conversationalist is often a terrific listener!

Suggested Activities

1. Give students the following assignment: Ask each other questions using words that start in order with the letters of the alphabet. For example:

   a. "Did you hear about the accident?"

   b. "Do you ever go bowling?"

   c. "How do you feel about cats?"

   d. "What is your favorite day of the week?"

   Ask students if this technique helped them feel more or less comfortable when talking to their classmates. What did they learn from this exercise?

2. Have students create masks that they can wear when talking to each other. Ask how wearing the masks affected their conversations.

Values and Character Skills Emphasized in This Discussion

- Confidence
- Positive Self-Esteem
- Communication

Topic 28: Not So Perfect

Issue for Discussion

I have a friend who everyone thinks is "perfect." He does everything right and never gets into trouble. I want to be more like my friend. What can I do?

Group Discussion of Possible Solutions

Is there really such a thing as "perfect"? Ask students to discuss the difficulties involved in trying to be "perfect." Have students differentiate "admirable" traits and "improvable" traits from "perfect." Follow up with this discussion: Nobody is perfect! We all do things that are good and we all do things that are not so good. Discuss with students the value of honoring who we are as we try to improve on those things about ourselves that could be better.

Suggested Activities

1. Have students make a list of things that make them feel proud. Discuss some of these things with the class.
2. Paste a small mirror on a piece of cardboard. Under this mirror place a strip of paper on which is written, "When I look in the mirror, I see someone who can ________________________________." Have students "visit" the mirror often.
3. Have students design a T-shirt on which they write or draw a picture of something that they do well or are proud of. Pin these T-shirts on a bulletin board so everyone can see why each member of the class is special.

Values and Character Skills Emphasized in This Discussion

- Confidence
- Positive Self-Esteem
- Responsibility to Self

Topic 29: Gym Class

Issue for Discussion

I hate going to gym class in school. I'm not very coordinated or athletic and I am embarrassed when I don't do well in class. What can I do?

Group Discussion of Possible Solutions

Ask students to discuss the value of gym class in school. Have students list the sports/activities they enjoy in gym class and the activities/sports they would rather ignore. Compare the different responses. Follow up with this discussion: Few people are gifted at every activity/sport—especially activities/sports in school. Gym class is intended to introduce students to a variety of sports, as well as offer opportunities to develop physical fitness. Talk to your gym teacher about your feelings. Talk, too, to a classmate who doesn't appear to have an aptitude for sports, but does seem to enjoy or have enthusiasm for gym class in school.

Suggested Activities

1. Invite a fitness trainer from a local health club to school to present an exercise program suitable for your students' age group. Ask the trainer to suggest exercises that will help improve your students' fitness.
2. Have students discuss the value of body fitness as it relates to state of mind and emotional well-being.

Values and Character Skills Emphasized in This Discussion

- Respect for One's Body
- Self-Discipline
- Perseverance

Topic 30: School Is Boring

Issue for Discussion

Some of my friends think school is boring. Sometimes I like school. Other times I think it's boring, too. Why is school so important?

Group Discussion of Possible Solutions

Ask students to list reasons why they think they go to school. Discuss with students what might happen to this country if its young people were not educated. Ask students to research the history of public education in this country—who received an education 100 years ago? 50 years ago? 25 years ago? Who receives an education today? Then follow up with this discussion: An educated citizenry is an investment in our country's future. Ask students to identify ways to take an active role in their learning and in their educations. How would they change the situation in school to make it seem less "boring"?

Suggested Activities

1. Ask students to identify ways to make school seem more exciting. Have students identify legitimate suggestions for improving their school experience and at the same time take responsibility for their learning.
2. Have students talk to parents, grandparents, aunts, and uncles and ask what advice they would give about school if they could do it all over again. Have students share the results of their informal interviews with the class.

Values and Character Skills Emphasized in This Discussion

- Perseverance
- Self-Discipline
- Citizenship

Topic 31: Stranger Danger

Issue for Discussion

I have learned both at home and in school not to go anywhere for any reason with a stranger. I'm older now and wonder if it is safe for me not to worry about this issue anymore. I feel I am old enough to take care of myself!

Group Discussion of Possible Solutions

Discuss with students the appropriate precautions to take with strangers—at any age (whether a child or an adult). Discuss the difference between safe and wise behavior and overly fearful behavior. Ask students to list safety behaviors they have learned over the years. Discuss the safety behaviors they have learned that have relevance regardless of one's age.

Suggested Activities

1. Have students suggest advice they would give a younger brother or sister about danger from strangers.
2. Have students role play potentially dangerous situations with strangers. Discuss safety behaviors and how to avoid risky situations.

Values and Character Skills Emphasized in This Discussion

- Self-Preservation
- Responsibility
- Problem Solving

Topic 32: No to Drugs and Smoking

Issue for Discussion

Some of my classmates at school smoke and/or use drugs. What am I supposed to say or do when these classmates want me to smoke/use drugs, too?

Group Discussion of Possible Solutions

Discuss with students the fact that drug use and smoking are on the rise among young people in our schools. Have students research the statistics on drug and cigarette use, as well as statistics citing the alarming consequences of drug use and smoking both in young people and over long-term use. Have students discuss and list ways to say "no" with confidence to drugs and/or smoking. Encourage students to begin a campaign in school against smoking and using drugs—"I choose not to smoke/use drugs" signs in the hallways, students who say no to smoking and drugs hall monitors, and so on.

Suggested Activities

1. Invite a local representative from a drug rehabilitation center to class to discuss the dangers of drug use and the value of saying "no" to drugs when students are young.
2. Invite a panel of former smokers to class to discuss the dangers of smoking and the consequences of starting smoking at an early age.

Values and Character Skills Emphasized in This Discussion

- Respect for Body
- Self-Preservation
- Positive Self-Esteem

Topic 33: The Right to Say "No"

Issue for Discussion

A friend asked me to do something I didn't feel comfortable doing—play a mean trick on a younger classmate. I told my friend "no." Now he is mad and won't even talk to me. What am I supposed to do?

Group Discussion of Possible Solutions

Ask students if they've ever done something they wished they had said "no" to. Ask how they felt when they went ahead and didn't say "no." Discuss the consequences of going against one's better judgment or values. Follow up with this discussion: Everyone has the right to say "no" to things that make them feel uncomfortable and the right to say "no" if "no" is an honest reaction to a request from another. Discuss with students how to be prepared to deal with the consequences of saying "no" to someone.

Suggested Activities

1. Have students role play saying "no" in a number of different situations.
2. Have students research several famous individuals who said "no" to different situations in their own courageous way.

Values and Character Skills Emphasized in This Discussion

- Respect for Self
- Honesty
- Independent Thinking

Topic 34: Inappropriate Behavior

Issue for Discussion

What should I do if someone says things to me or behaves around me in ways that make me feel uncomfortable?

Group Discussion of Possible Solutions

Discuss with students what to do when behaviors and language feel inappropriate to them. Ask students to identify positive solutions to inappropriate language and behaviors. Discuss with students the necessity of sharing information about inappropriate language or behaviors with a trusted adult. Discuss, too, the importance of trusting their feelings about what is and isn't appropriate.

Suggested Activities

1. Invite a counselor to class to talk about students' rights and what to do when students feel uncomfortable about someone's behavior or language.
2. Have students dramatize the issue of trusting their feelings.

Values and Character Skills Emphasized in This Discussion

- Positive Self-Esteem
- Self-Preservation
- Moral Awareness

Topic 35: New Roles for Girls and Women

Issue for Discussion

I know the roles for girls and women are changing, but I sometimes get mixed messages about what I can do and how I should act in certain situations. What am I supposed to do?

Group Discussion of Possible Solutions

Ask students to research how the roles for girls and women have changed over the last 100 years. How have they changed over the last 20 years? Discuss with students reasons why the roles may have changed. List, too, the positive and negative effects of some of these changes. Discuss why girls and women may be getting mixed messages about their new roles in business, in society, and in family. Discuss legal and societal changes that have led to and encouraged important role changes.

Suggested Activities

1. Ask students to list for themselves goals/opportunities that have nothing to do with being male or female. Discuss whether these goals are achievable and the obstacles that may surface and need to be dealt with along the way.
2. Have students write character sketches of a girl's/woman's role fifty years ago vs. character sketches of a girl's/woman's role in the 21st century.

Values and Character Skills Emphasized in This Discussion

- Tolerance for Diversity
- Respect
- Cooperation

Topic 36: New Roles for Boys and Men

Issue for Discussion

Roles for boys and men are also changing. How do I know what I should and can do and what I can expect as I get older?

Group Discussion of Possible Solutions

Ask students to research how the roles for boys and men have changed over the last 20 years. Discuss with students what these role changes mean for boys and men. Ask students to evaluate how changing roles for boys/men and girls/women affect all aspects of society. How do changes in society affect the roles of boys/men and girls/women?

Suggested Activities

1. Ask students to evaluate how changes in technology have affected changes in roles for both men and women. Have students imagine how future changes may affect other role changes for both genders.
2. Have students write character sketches of a boy's/man's role fifty years ago vs. character sketches of a boy's/man's role in the 21st century.

Values and Character Skills Emphasized in This Discussion

- Tolerance for Diversity
- Respect
- Cooperation

Topic 37: Learning to Win or Lose with Style

Issue for Discussion

When I lose, whether it's a game or something else, I get mad or very upset. My friends say I'm a sore loser. Am I? What can I do to change how I react?

Group Discussion of Possible Solutions

Ask students what it feels like to lose a game. Ask what it feels like to win. Have students discuss political candidates, athletes, actors/actresses who have won or lost elections, games, or awards. Show videotapes of gracious winners and gracious losers. Discuss with students the value of winning and losing with style.

Suggested Activities

1. Have students role play situations of losing for the class. Discuss the consequences of a poor loser.
2. Have students "interview" a variety of fictitious "winners" in a talk-show format. Ask some students to be braggarts and others to be gracious winners. After the interviews, discuss the effect on the audience of both types of winners.

Values and Character Skills Emphasized in This Discussion

- Empathy
- Optimism
- Teamwork

Topic 38: Diversity Issues

Issue for Discussion

I sometimes see students in my school treat other students badly only because they are different—from different countries, of different races, wearing different clothes, and so on. I also see different groups angry or fighting with each other. What should I do?

Group Discussion of Possible Solutions

Have students list the diverse backgrounds of the many students in their school—Hispanic, Black, Asian, Russian, Midwestern, Eastern, living in the country, living in the city, etc. Discuss the positive effects of this diversity on the school. Discuss, too, the difficulties that may arise as a result of this diversity. Follow up with the following discussion: People from all over the world live in the United States. In fact, many legal immigrants become United States citizens every year. Discuss with students the responsibility we all have to each other as U.S. citizens. Discuss, too, tangible suggestions for valuing and appreciating and respecting our differences in a way that helps us get along and work together.

Suggested Activities

1. Have students work together at school to encourage a community that respects diversity—signs in the hall, school-sponsored diversity projects, etc.
2. Invite representatives from local businesses that are racially diverse to speak to the class about the importance of valuing diversity in this country.

Values and Character Skills Emphasized in This Discussion

- Fairness
- Conflict Resolution
- Tolerance for Diversity

Topic 39: Worried

Issue for Discussion

Sometimes I have trouble doing well in school because I'm worried about something that is bothering me. What can I do?

Group Discussion of Possible Solutions

Talk with students about how difficult it is to concentrate on something when we are troubled about other issues. Ask students to suggest ways for relieving stress and worries. Talk to friends. Talk to teachers. Talk to a counselor. Talk to parents or another trusted adult. Encourage students to openly discuss their concerns with someone. Everyone at one time or another will have worries that concern them. It's best to talk about the problems with trusted friends or family members.

Suggested Activities

1. Have students use puppets to role play solutions to a variety of stressful situations.
2. Encourage students to keep a private journal where thoughts, concerns, and worries can be expressed or written.

Values and Character Skills Emphasized in This Discussion

- Communication
- Problem Solving
- Respect for Authority

Topic 40: Feeling Good About Myself

Issue for Discussion

I sometimes think I'm stupid. I sometimes think I'm ugly. What can I do to feel better about myself?

Group Discussion of Possible Solutions

Pair students with a partner. Then have each partner list three adjectives that describe the other person on a sheet of paper. Ask each student to also list three adjectives that describe themselves. Have partners share their adjectives with one another. Follow up with the following discussion: We all have things about ourselves that are positive. We all have things about ourselves that could change. Ask students to think about the adjectives they and their partners came up with about themselves. Solicit suggestions from all students about positive tips for improving self-esteem and feeling good about themselves. Talk especially about minimizing the number of "bad" messages students give themselves and encourage increasing the number of "positive" messages. In short, encourage students to "give themselves a break."

Suggested Activities

1. Encourage students to write complimentary and humorous poems about one another that celebrate each individual. Share the poems.
2. Have students create a chart of tips for feeling good about themselves. Post the chart in the classroom or in several places in the hallways at school.

Values and Character Skills Emphasized in This Discussion

- Confidence
- Positive Self-Esteem
- Caring